Eileen Hirst

Start Up

Stay Up

A guide to the Financial & Legal

aspects of becoming

Self-Employed or Starting a Business

Eileen Hirst

Introduction

At the end of 2019, over 5 million people in the UK were classed as self-employed. They represented 15.3% of all people in work. (Office for National
Statistics - ONS)
Self-employed people are those who define themselves as working for themselves, rather than receiving a wage or salary from an employer.
The majority are registered as self-employed and include start-ups, small businesses, freelancers, partnerships and subcontractors.
The highest numbers are in the construction industry, approximately two thirds of the self-employed are male, and 10% are over 65 years of age.

In a 2017 ONS report, researchers had looked at the reasons given for self-employment. Their findings were as follows:
Positive reasons: a) A person saw the demand in the market. b) Self-employment was the nature of the
person's job or career choice. c) Better working conditions or job satisfaction were foreseen to be the result of self-employment.

Negative reasons: a) Redundancy. b) Inability to find other employment.

Redundancy was stated as a reason by mainly older workers and a small share of part-time self-employed young men said they made the choice under difficult circumstances, especially economic hardship.

Lifestyle choice: a) To maintain or increase income. b) To create a job after retirement - younger women looking for flexibility figured largely here.

Neutral reasons: Where a person started or joined a family business.

The study found that the *full-time, self-employed sector* remains highly skewed towards men. It found that these people work between 50 and 70 hours per week as opposed to the 35 to 45 hours of those in employment. A third of the group are located in the South East and London. The sector is composed of mainly people working in skilled trades, especially construction and financial and business services.

Eileen Hirst

About this book

If you are reading this you are presumably considering self-employment or are thinking of or started a business. You might be baffled by the regulations, especially those relating to tax and National Insurance.

Whether it's full-time or part-time self-employment you are entering, you need to be aware of the legal aspects of business. You will find them included in this easy guide. It's regularly updated to include the latest tax allowances and covers the answers to questions that concern most start-ups, including:

How do I register my business?

What is Self-Assessment?

How much tax and National Insurance will I pay?

Should I become a Limited Company?

Do I need an Accountant?

What records must I keep?

What about legal issues such as insurance, Health and Safety, bad debts, business names............ and so on.

Do I need a Business Bank Account?

How do I know if my business will bring me in enough money to live on?

Where can I get grants or loans from?

What is a business plan? Do I need one and how could I get help in drawing one up?

About The Author

When you've finished reading this book you will have a great overview of how to start a legal and financially solid business.

How do I know this? I know this because I have a business - I work for myself - and part of what I do is training start-ups. I have used feedback from my workshops to determine what to include in the book and I've selected the information that clients find most useful and helpful. This book is a summary of the workshops. It answers the questions most start-ups ask and can be used to complement any other source of help and advice you might receive. It also includes interviews with people who have started their own business or become self-employed. Everyone included in this book is still in business after almost ten years - and they all started with very little funding.

As well as knowing the rules of business you should also be aware of the pitfalls. Ignorance will not save you when creditors (including, and especially, the taxman) come knocking at your door. Spending a short time to familiarise yourself with the basics will.

Read on and discover how to start a business or become self-employed, successfully. After that, as Christine Anne Rowlands says in one of the Case Studies, 'you learn as you go along.'

Chapter 1: Thinking about starting up

Starting up and staying up

An entrepreneur is someone who organises, operates, and assumes the risks of a business or enterprise. As a start-up, you are (or are about to become) such a person. Business is a progressive journey and your starting point must always be consideration of the market you're looking to enter. If that market is already crammed with successful providers, you'll struggle to make money from it – unless you offer customers something different, something that is more valuable to them.

Before you dive in, invest in premises, a van and stock and so on, look closely at your market. Speak to people, including your competitors, and listen to what they tell you.

There is always competition - people out there offering what you are thinking of selling or an alternative. Maybe they're not exactly on your doorstep, but that could be because there isn't the demand in your local area. Where competition is strong, it will be difficult to start a profitable business. Customers tend to stick with suppliers they're used to; they might try a one-off transaction elsewhere but you need repeat customers to stay in business.

On the other hand, if you find that your competitors are not so good and that you could do better, there may be a gap in the market. Only by speaking to people, listening, and observing your competitors in action, will you find the true market situation. It takes time and patience, it's known as 'market research' and will give you a far better chance of survival than if you throw yourself in without direction or planning.

After studying the market you will need to examine your business skills (as opposed to your personal skills).

Most people have little idea of how to run a business initially and without the right advice and support it's easy to run into trouble in the early days – even Richard Branson spent a night in a police cell for contravening the VAT regulations. Be honest with yourself; identify your business-related strengths and weaknesses and look at what help is available to you.

The UK Government provides free-of-charge advice and support for start-ups, both online and offline and through different agencies. Her Majesty's Revenue & Customs (HMRC) – the tax and VAT people – maintain a comprehensive website, www.hmrc.gov.uk, which holds the information you need. They also offer a wide-range of workshops to help you start and grow your business.

The government wants you to start a business. It wants you to be financially self-sufficient and, if possible, to grow your business and create employment for others. To this end, they offer you help and advice from qualified and experienced business professionals.

Once you have examined your business skills and highlighted any areas that you need to work on, you should look at your resources – time and money. Each new business will have start-up requirements and would-be-entrepreneurs tend to produce a list of ideals - a vehicle, premises, equipment...... that their limited resources will never run to. There's no reason not to draw up this list, as long as you realise that it will probably have to be trimmed.

A considerable backdrop of money for day-to-day running expenses is necessary in the early stages of a business and this is often missing from the list. Customers will take a while to come on board, and when they do their initial sales will be small. They'll try you out, test you, and in the first few weeks and months you need a cash reserve to survive.

Most start-ups borrow money to fund their

businesses. Government agencies offer start-up loans at competitive rates of interest and they should be your first port of call if you are looking for finance. The banks want to assist businesses too. In practice though, it is more difficult and costly for a start-up to obtain finance from them because a new business has no trading history and cannot demonstrate that it's credit worthy. The bank interest rates on loans will be higher and the conditions more stringent. However, an ethical Bank Manager will always direct a client towards a government loan fund if he or she can't help you, so the banks *are* worth approaching at start-up.

We'll look at borrowing in more detail later. It's a huge commitment and 'bootstrapping' – where a person starts up with little or no institutional borrowing – is the modern alternative. Bootstrappers trim their ideal start-up equipment list and look at the minimum they can manage with. Then they make do, or borrow from family and friends rather than fund their business through expensive loans.

Finally, there is the profitability of your business venture to consider. You must be able to sell for more money than you buy for, and cover your operating costs - that's the bottom line! Not only should the profit cover all your costs, it should also leave you with enough to pay your taxes and to live on. Draw up a personal budget statement and ask yourself if you will be able to survive on the profit you've estimated. If the return is not enough, you should rethink your idea.

Business plans are the start-up's blueprint. They are designed to show whether or not your idea is likely to pay off. Yes, you can start off with £100, buy stock, and then resell it at a profit like in 'The Apprentice' - that will get you off the starting block. But to be consistently profitable and to manage your cash flow over a long period of time, it's more complicated. Well-researched, planned approaches to business more than double your chances of success.

How is self-employment different from employment?

The main difference between working for yourself and working for an employer is that you are responsible for everything.

If you've previously been employed, your employer took care of you - paid your wages, sent off your tax and National Insurance, made sure that the business operated safely and legally, that it was adequately insured......and found enough customers to survive. There was, perhaps, a Sales and Marketing department, Finance and Human

Resource experts - specialists dealing with the essential aspects of running a business.

Start-ups have no such structure. The business owner has sole responsibility if anything goes wrong. Because of this, many people see setting up in business as daunting. This is why the government steps in to help out.

Where to find start-up help and advice:
Enterprise Agencies

For people with a business idea, sub-contractors, or the self-employed, the nearest Enterprise Agency should be your first port of call. You can search for yours at www.gov.uk/starting-up-a-business/start-with-an-idea, or at www.nationalenterprisenetwork.org.

Enterprise Agencies have Business Advisers and Trainers who specialise in working with start-up and growth businesses. They provide workshops and one-to-one advice sessions to get you up and running with your research and then they help you to create a business plan. They are also often aware of any grants or subsidised loans available.

Government Agencies provide excellent support for start-ups. Even if they cannot offer you finance, they will help you in other ways. You're likely to find that spending time with their advisers and start-ups like yours can be motivating in itself.

Banks

All of the High Street banks have a business department dealing with start-ups. Banks have money to lend to businesses – after all, they make most of their money from lending – but bank lending will always be subject to specific criteria and will be expensive for a start-up with no track record. Banks and other lenders all want to see a business plan before considering a request for funding; another reason to visit one of the government agencies before you start.

Chapter 2: Which type of business structure should you choose? How do you register your business and how does the tax system work?

Her Majesty's Revenue & Customs (HMRC)

As mentioned previously, HMRC is the official Government Agency responsible for collecting tax, National Insurance and VAT. When you are employed, your employer calculates your tax and National Insurance and sends it to HMRC for you. However, when you start a business or work for yourself, you have to deal with them directly. Your first responsibility is to tell them that you have started – to register your self-employment. You must enrol for Self Assessment (see below) by the 5th October in the year **following** the one you started up in. Before registering, you need to consider which type of business to set up.

Legal Business Formats

There are a variety of business models – known as legal business formats - for you to choose from when you start up. All of them are regulated by HMRC and are packaged under the following headings:

·Sole Trader
·Partnership
·Limited Company
·Social Enterprise

Each model has different legal implications and you'll have to choose which one is the most appropriate for your business. The information below will help you do this.

Sole Trader

The simplest way for an individual to start up is as a Sole Trader. This model covers self-employed people, sub-contractors, freelancers and the owner/managers of start-up businesses.

The system HMRC uses to collect taxes from Sole Traders is known as 'Self Assessment'. We'll look at that shortly.

Advantages of starting up as a Sole Trader:

It's simple and free to register your business online, by phone, or in person.

Self Assessment is comparatively simple in terms of paperwork and you do not legally have to use an accountant

If your business idea does not work out, you can submit your figures and inform HMRC that you have ceased to trade

It suits part-time businesses and sub-contractors and can be combined with full or part-time employment

You can change from Sole Trader status to that of a Limited Company if your business grows and it becomes advantageous tax-wise

Partnerships

Where two or more people work together in the same business, they may decide to form a partnership.

Partnerships pay taxes to HMRC in the same way as Sole Traders - through the Self Assessment system. They are easy to set up - you don't have to have an accountant - but you should have a legal Partnership Agreement in place that sets out the terms and agreed responsibilities for the partners; for example, on dissolution.

Limited Companies

Limited Companies are another legal structure for start-up businesses and the self-employed. Comprehensive information is available at www.gov.uk/running-a-limited-company/directors-responsibilities

Companies are regulated by HMRC (through Companies House) and generally benefit growing businesses. They have more legal obligations and bureaucracy to handle than a Sole Trader, are more expensive to maintain because their accounts have to be audited annually by an accountant, and their accounts are open to the public, for a small fee, on the Companies House website. This means that the information about a company is much more transparent – readily available for viewing - than that of a Sole Trader or Partnership.

One of the benefits of a limited company is that it is a separate legal entity in its own right. It can sue or be sued (taken to court if things go wrong) because it is considered to be a body or person in the eyes of the law - just like you or me. Whilst this might seem attractive (in that if things go wrong you could walk away unscathed) in practice, when you buy a limited company (see later) you become its director and, as such, have legal obligations which will almost always prevent this happening.

Social Enterprises

Social or Community Enterprises are similar to Limited Companies in the way they are formed and Regulated, but are specialist in nature. They are formed by enterprises with objectives related to helping people or communities and can take the following forms: Limited Companies; Charitable Incorporated Organisations (CIO's); Co-operatives; Community Interest Companies (CIC's); Sole Traders or Business Partnerships. www.gov.uk/setupasocialenterprise. Again, their accounts must be audited by an accountant and made available to interested parties.

Registering as a Sole Trader

As soon as you take money from someone you have done work for, either sold them a product or carried out a service, you have a potential tax liability.

You can register online (see below) or by telephone - look in your local telephone directory for the number – or you can visit your nearest Tax Office.

As the majority of people now register online, we'll go through that process here. If you register by phone, or in person, you will need to provide the same information to whoever you speak to.

Registering online

Go to the website www.gov.uk/set-up-sole-trader/register/

Click on 'registering as a new business' and follow the process.

Registration will take at least 10 working days, you need an activation code to access the Government Gateway and set up your account. The code will be sent by post and after that you will be able to complete the process online.

To register for Self Assessment (the tax and National Insurance system for the self-employed) you will simply input personal information, including your name, National Insurance number and an e-mail address. When this is complete, your legal obligation is fulfilled. You won't hear anything from HMRC until sometime after the following April when you will receive your Self Assessment Tax Return (SA100).

Self Assessment Returns

Self-Assessment Returns are sent out to Sole Traders and Partnerships in April each year.

On this return you are asked to state your sales and business expenses for the year. Business expenses* include the cost of any stock you've bought and any business invoices you've paid (more of this later). When you deduct the expenses from your sales figure, the difference is either a Profit or a Loss. Tax and National Insurance will only be charged if you have made a profit, and losses can sometimes be carried forward to the next tax year.

*One of the benefits of being in business is that you are able to claim for certain expenses before you are taxed.

Sole traders pay their taxes in two annual instalments on the 31st January and 31st July each year. They do not pay monthly or weekly as employed people do. This means that self-employed people have to estimate how much tax and National Insurance they need to set aside for when their payments are due. Saving for your taxes is crucial. HMRC employ ruthless debt collectors who will pursue you and close you down if you do not conform to their rules and regulations.

Some people (especially accountants) will advise you to find an accountant as soon as you start. It is true that a good one can save you money (by reducing your tax bill) but they will charge you for their services and watching your money is very important when you start a business. If you can grasp the basics of the tax system from reading this book, you will be able to estimate how much you should be saving for your tax and National Insurance as you go along. If you don't feel it's something you can get to grips with, don't worry; it's important to have some understanding of the process, even if someone else does the calculating for you.

Because of start-up costs, new businesses don't tend to pay too much tax initially. In fact, until they become established and their sales take off, start-ups and sub-contractors often get tax refunds in their early years.

Tax Year End

To complete your Self Assessment Tax Return you will need a record of any money you have taken from customers for sales and for any business expenses you have paid out.

For the forthcoming tax years, if your sales are below £85,000, as well as completing your personal information you will only have to fill in a 'three-line-account' on your annual Self Assessment Return.

The three lines are:

SALES

EXPENSES

PROFIT/LOSS

These three figures are important, not only because they appear on your tax return, but also because they measure how well your business is performing. They represent the magic formula for business success. Profit after tax is what you're looking for – you are in this to make money for yourself as well as sending the information to the tax office.

People are always curious about what constitutes a business expense. The idea of off-setting your expenses and thereby paying less tax is always attractive. Business expenses are any costs that you incur in making your sales happen or in operating the day-to-day running of your business. They are covered in more detail when we look at book-keeping and by that time you will have an understanding of how the tax system works. Just remember that, right from the start of your business - even at the market research stage - you should keep any receipts for business expenses and note down any car mileage or travel expenses that you incur.

Employed and Self-employed

If you are both employed and self-employed, you may have paid tax and National Insurance though an employer. If so, a P60 will be issued by your employer in April and the information from it should be included on your tax return. Any profit or loss from your business or self-employment will be combined with your employed earnings and deductions - before HMRC finalise your annual tax figure and notify you of it.

So, three lines and your personal information and your Self Assessment Return is complete. HMRC will take it from there. They will inform you of any tax and National Insurance owed or refundable.

Sales over £85,000

When your sales reach around £85,000 in any one year, the Government requires more detailed information about your business expenses. It is still relatively easy to complete the Self Assessment Return - the only difference is that HMRC will expect you to analyse your expenses into certain standard categories. These include; premises, administration, wages, motor expenses, and advertising. It means that, as your business grows, your book-keeping system will have to become more detailed.

The threshold for VAT is currently set at sales of £85,000 per annum and this has further implications for tax and book-keeping. We'll look at VAT shortly.

Many small businesses do not expect to make sales of over £85,000 in their first year and, whilst it is important to understand tax and VAT, the focus at the start of your business should be on acquiring and retaining customers. Initially you will probably only have to produce a three line account for HMRC and you will have plenty of time to get used to keeping more detailed records. By the time you reach the VAT limit, you will in all likelihood have employed an accountant or a book-keeper to help you with your records.

Setting money aside for your tax and National Insurance

Disputes with HMRC are time-consuming and frustrating. When you start out, it's usually quite a while before you have to pay any taxes or National Insurance. Take, for example, a business that starts in May. The owner will not receive a Self Assessment Return until April of the following year (a whole eleven months later). If he or she owes any tax, it will not become payable until the end of the following January (twenty months later). This is a long time and not spending the money you've set aside is difficult. You have to become disciplined. Start your records from the very beginning and set aside the money from sales. HMRC will calculate what you owe, but you must have the cash to pay.

Experienced business people (especially those who have failed in a previous attempt) always set aside a proportion of their sales income (usually around 20-25%) to cover their taxes, as soon as it comes in. You will receive interest on the money if you place it in a deposit account, so make sure you do this - failure to pay taxes has closed down many otherwise successful businesses.

How taxes and National Insurances are calculated

Everyone in this country is entitled to a Personal Allowance - an annual amount of earnings or profit which is free from tax and National Insurance.

For the year commencing April 2020/21 this amount is £12,500. (In 2019/20 it was also £12,500).

When you are employed, your employer allocated you a proportion of this allowance each payday before calculating your tax and National Insurance. However, when you work for yourself, your tax bill is calculated annually, rather than weekly or monthly. Your total Personal Allowance is taken away from your annual profit and tax is charged on the remainder.

For example, if your profit for the year is £15,000, your annual Personal Allowance of £12,500 will be deducted from it before tax is calculated on the remaining £2,500.

The basic rate of tax is 20%. This means that on £2,500 profit you will be charged £500. If your business has made a profit below the Personal Allowance of £12,500, or a loss, no tax will be due.

From April 2020, the higher tax rate of 40% is charged on any profit above £50,000. (In 2019/20 it was £37,500). Please note that any profit below these figures is charged at the 20% basic rate, the higher rate only applies to profit above them.

This is not something that should concern the majority of start-ups because, if it looks from the outset that your business will reach high profits in the first year, you will probably form a limited company rather than start as a sole trader. Companies have a different tax structure and offer certain breaks to those with higher profits (more later).

Now for the unexpected taxes you have to watch out for!

National Insurance for the Self-Employed

There are currently different types of National Insurance. The names are historical and unimportant from a business perspective, but you need to be aware of them. Once you understand them, view them all as taxes - i.e. money you pay to the government via HMRC.

Class 2 National Insurance

This is charged weekly, entitles you to benefits, and contributes towards your State Pension.

For 2020 the cost is £3.05 per week (In 2019/20 it was £3) and the year's charge will be added to your taxes when your Self Assessment Return is processed.

Not everyone will pay Class 2 National Insurance for the following reasons:

If you are working for an employer and you are also self-employed, you may be paying enough Class 1 National

Insurance (National Insurance for employed persons) through your wages to cover your Class 2 liability.

If your business is small and this year makes a profit of less than £6,475 (£6,365 in 2019/20) you can apply for exemption from Class 2 National Insurance.

If you are at, or nearing, State Pension age and have paid National Insurance throughout your working life, you may have enough contributions recorded already. You can request a Pension Forecast online and find your current position.

Class 4 National Insurance

This is National Insurance charged on the profits of the self-employed and is in addition to Class 2.

In 2020 Class 4 National Insurance at a rate of 9% will charged on any profit between £9,500 and £50,000. (In 2019/20 it was between £8,632 and £50,000). Again, this is in addition to the basic rate of tax and your Class 2 National Insurance.

If this shocks you, or seems unfair, consider the amount of Class 1 National Insurance - around 12% - that employed people pay in comparison. Also it is important to remember that the 9% Class 4 National Insurance is only payable on profit greater than £9,500.

For many start-ups, the tax and National Insurance you are charged will not be huge amounts of money initially. You must get used to saving for them though. Set aside regular amounts of money – 25% of any sales income will take you a long way towards meeting your charges and you might have some left over.

Paying your tax and National Insurance

There is one final hurdle you need to be aware of when paying taxes for the self-employed.

As stated at the beginning of this section, when you register your business you will have up to 18 months (for April start-ups) before you pay any tax or National Insurance.

Employed people pay tax and National Insurance regularly through the Pay as You Earn (PAYE) system, the employer deducting it weekly or monthly. Because the self-employed pay annually, and in arrears, HMRC demand a Payment on Account for the following year, with your first tax assessment. Here is an example of how such a payment is calculated:

If your tax and National Insurance for your first year in self-employment is, for example, £2,000, HMRC will charge you an additional £1,000 (50%) as a payment on account for the following year. This means your final assessment becomes £3,000, payable in two instalments on the 31st January and the 31st July of the following year.

The Payment-on-Account is a one-off charge in your first year of self-employment. In subsequent years it is adjusted up or down in accordance with the year's profit or loss.

You might have to read the previous paragraphs several times – it is difficult to get your head around tax, National Insurance and Payments-on-Account.

It's easy to see how start-ups get into trouble with HMRC. Being prepared, by setting aside money for taxes, is the only way to survive. A simple way of doing this is, as mentioned earlier, to ignore the different taxes and allowances and set aside 25% of your sales takings from the outset. Whilst this is not exact, it will get you into the habit of saving and make a large contribution towards your first tax assessment.

If you choose to, you can pay in advanced instalments to HMRC by monthly Direct Debit. They will set you up a Budget Payment Plan (BPP) and allow you to discontinue payments for up to six months if you find they've overestimated your liability.

A final word of warning to those who remain employed or part-time employed, and set up in self-employment. Employers allocate your Personal Allowance through the PAYE system and if you use it up through your wages, you will be liable for the full 20% tax and 9% National Insurance on your self-employed profits.

Partnerships

Quite often two or more people get together and work on a partnership basis. There can be advantages in terms of sharing workloads and experience and a partnership might be seen as an attractive proposition. Here's how it works.

Registering a Partnership with HMRC

The system for registration with HMRC is the same as for Sole Traders. Both or all partners register separately and then the business is registered as a partnership.

Partnership Agreements

There are potential pitfalls when you work as a partnership. These need to be planned for in advance and set out in a partnership agreement.

Partnerships do not last not forever, circumstances change. In the worst case scenario, if a partner dies, the business bank account is frozen. Similarly, if a partner becomes personally bankrupt, the bank account is closed. For reasons such as these, a legal agreement is worth spending time and money on at the outset.

There are several areas that commonly lead to disputes and these are covered in such a document.

They include:

Paying interest on the capital introduced into the business by each partner. This will often differ and can become a cause of dissatisfaction unless some form of recompense is agreed.

Level of drawings (money each partner takes out as wages). Once again, if not agreed in advance, it can lead to ill-feeling.

Dissolution of the partnership; how its assets and liabilities are to be shared.

Any legal agreement should be checked by a

solicitor to ensure it will stand up in a court of law in the event of dispute. Legal advice is expensive and any advance preparation will save you money. Download a sample Partnership Agreement and adapt it for your business, before seeing a solicitor. You will then be confident about what you are agreeing on and hopefully save on costs.

Finally, it's worth mentioning that a couple may be attracted by the idea of combining both of their Personal Allowances and working in one business. If you choose to do this, bear in mind that the sales from the business need to be high enough to provide decent return for two people.

Self-Assessment and Year End Returns for Partnerships

Again, the system is the same as for Sole Traders. A Self-Assessment Return is submitted to HMRC each year with the combined sales and expenses of all the partners. The Personal Allowance for each of the partners is deducted from the profit before any tax and Class 4 National Insurance is calculated. Class 2 National Insurance is, this year, charged for each partner.

Limited Companies

One of the major decisions you have to make when starting a business is whether to set up as a sole trader or a limited company. The choice is entirely yours, so let's look at the advantages of both.

A sole trader has less paperwork and lower costs than a limited company. Also certain individuals (the general public) might prefer to deal with an individual rather than a company.

A limited company can minimise risk, be more tax efficient, make it easier to obtain financial backing, and can portray a more professional image.

Let's look at limited companies in more detail because, although they look attractive, for many of the self-employed it might not be the best option.

Limited Liability

A limited company is a separate legal entity which can sue or be sued (taken to court if things go wrong). It is a body or a person in the eyes of the law - just like we are. They are cheap and easy to set up – there are a multitude of company formation sites advertising on the internet.

However, whilst it is as simple and as cheap as it appears to purchase a limited company, in terms of administration, costs, paperwork and bureaucracy, and the practical duties of becoming a company director, it is more time-consuming and costly than starting out as a sole trader.

When you buy a limited company and become the director of it, you have legal obligations. Company accounts must be filed annually through Companies House (HMRC for companies) and they must be audited by an accountant to show that they display a true and fair view of the company's financial position. The accountant also reports on shareholders and the Annual General Meeting to show that everything has been carried out legally.

A genuine reason for forming a company is because of the 'limited liability' it offers. Limited liability means that, because the company is a separate legal body, if is ever unable to pay its creditors (persons or businesses the company owes money to) they have to sue the company, rather than the owner, to recover the debt. The director is not held personally liable providing he or she has complied with the legal duties of a director. If a company cannot pay its debts and is declared bankrupt, its assets (what it owns) can be seized by the creditor and the director can technically walk away without losing any of his or her personal assets. Obviously this looks like a great advantage and it's not surprising that people start out thinking they'll set up a company for this reason, but in practice, banks, investors and creditors will not lend you money just because you own a company. They will still require some form of security from you in case you cannot meet your payments. A new company without assets cannot offer them this. If your company owns a building, or a fleet of vehicles, it's a different matter. If it owns nothing substantial, like many start-ups, then a creditor will always ask you for a personal guarantee - a loan secured against your own personal assets such as your home.

You can change from sole trader status to that of a limited company at any time. As your business grows and acquires assets, having a company that holds them will allow banks and investors to consider you more favourably. Successful start-ups tend to grow into limited companies, but do not register your start-up as a company until you are certain that it is beneficial. If it's having a company name that appeals to you, you can buy the company and leave it dormant until you require it.

As to the expense of having a company, an accountant will charge you a minimum of £500 +VAT (£600) to complete a set of accounts (as opposed to around

£200 for those of a sole trader). Your accountancy fees are classed as a business expense and, as such, are tax deductible. But ask yourself if committing to £600+ is sensible at the outset. You will have to pay it whether or not you make a profit.

Other reasons for forming a company

Sometimes businesses have to be limited companies in order to tender for contracts. Public and Local Authorities or large corporations often prefer to work with companies as they can to search for information about them on the government website: www.companieshouse.gov.uk

It's impossible with sole traders; there are millions of people registered with HMRC and their figures are never disclosed.

From a marketing point of view, and depending on the field of business you work in, a limited company profile can portray a bigger image. Again, when your resources are limited, it's an item on your start-up checklist that requires evaluation.

Filing Accounts at Year End

Limited companies choose their own year-end date. They do not have to file their accounts with Companies House in April, although many of them do to stay in line with the government's tax year.

For small limited companies, HMRC requires the same information as for sole traders - Sales, Expenses (broken down into categories) and Profit or Loss. There are however, differences in the way company taxation is calculated.

Calculating Tax & National Insurance for Limited Companies

Corporation tax – paid by companies – is more complex than self-assessment. A good accountant will guide you through the process, complete the calculations and file your company's accounts. This is how it operates in brief:

The current rate of tax on profits is 19%.

There is no charge for Class 4 National Insurance; however, as a director and employee of the company you are liable for Class 1 National Insurance on any wages you pay yourself above the Personal Allowance.

In addition to taking a wage, you are allowed to pay yourself dividends from any profit you have made (and don't want to leave in reserve in the company). These are taxed separately on a personal basis. The first £2,000 is tax free and the basic rate of tax on dividends is 7.5% with a higher rate of 32.5% (www.gov.uk/tax-on-dividends).

Social Enterprises

Social Enterprises are mainly set up for community-based projects, for example, where a group of people are awarded lottery funding. A legal structure is required to protect and regulate both the recipients of the monies (usually they form a committee) and the financiers.

The set-up process is similar to that of a limited company - an accountant who specialises in social enterprises is required from the outset and audited accounts have to be submitted annually to HMRC.

Unlike a limited company, the directors are salaried and profits remain within the enterprise. The legalities are documented and a Board of Directors is appointed to oversee them.

It will be clear by now that there are a variety of legal formats to consider when you start up. Each has its own specific advantages and disadvantages.

A business plan sets out in writing a financial

forecast of sales and expenses based on the business's goals. We'll look at how to draw one up in subsequent chapters, but if you have this information from the start, it will be easier for you to decide which legal format best fits your needs.

Generally speaking, it's easier and cheaper to start as a sole trader. When your business grows, discuss your position with an accountant – usually when you look to be approaching the £85,000 sales mark in any one year.

There is no right or wrong way, as long as you stick to HMRC's rules. Your personal vision and goals will also determine how you proceed.

Value Added Tax (VAT)

VAT is a tax that applies to any business with sales of £85,000 and over (In 2016 it was £83,000) - irrespective of their legal format.

Registering for VAT

The VAT threshold, the level at which you are legally obliged to register for VAT, is currently £85,000 sales in any one year. When your business reaches this level of sales (not profit) you must register with HMRC and start charging and accounting for any VAT that you receive from customers. You can also reclaim any VAT that you pay out to suppliers or for business expenses.

Certain businesses are exempt from VAT; generally speaking this is where the business sells essential products such as food and medicine or offers essential services such as nursing care. It is easy to check on the HMRC website to find out whether or not VAT applies to your business sector.

How the VAT system works

From the date your business is registered for VAT, 20% of your sales income has to be paid at regular intervals to HMRC (usually monthly or quarterly). Any VAT the business pays out for stock or expenses can be reclaimed against this income.

As the sales income of a business is higher than its expenses, most businesses will pay the net difference once they have registered. Start-ups selling expensive products or services are likely to reach the VAT limit in their first year and must register. For others, when it is apparent that they will hit the threshold in that particular trading year, they must notify HMRC.

Will VAT affect your start-up?

A business plan will show you whether or not you will reach the VAT threshold in your first year. Without a business plan, you will have to monitor your sales closely and as soon as it looks as though you might reach the threshold, you must register.

Being prepared for VAT is particularly important because you cannot suddenly increase your sales prices by twenty per cent. Customers can always turn to competitors with lower prices (including other start-ups that have not yet reached the threshold).

If your business takes off and appears likely to reach £85,000 sales in any trading year, look for ways to add value to your existing customers and then gradually increase your selling prices.

Completing a VAT Return

VAT registration is a growth step for any business and, as stated earlier, when your business grows to around £85k in sales, it is advisable to see an accountant.

Your book-keeping will need to be adjusted to comply with the VAT Return requirements (digital records are required when submitting a return, see www.gov.uk/vat-record-keeping/making-tax-digital-for-vat, and there are various schemes available for small businesses, such as the flat rate scheme, that might be of benefit to you. HMRC run free workshops covering start-up and all the major growth stages of a business, including VAT registration.

Reaching the VAT threshold is particularly significant for businesses that sell to the public as opposed to those that sell to other businesses. This is because, if you're selling to other businesses and they are VAT registered, they can reclaim the tax you charge them. The general

public can't and they might look for a competitor who isn't registered, if you pass the cost onto them.

This is not a reason to stop growing your business – unless you want to. There are many VAT registered businesses that thrive because they've grown and are able to absorb costs (buy creating better purchasing opportunities, for example). It's largely down to your own personal and business objectives; just plan and prepare before you're forced into it.

It's time for a break from the 'do's and don'ts' and the rules and regulations. By now you're probably wondering why anyone starts a business. Let's look at two start-ups, still in business ten years on.

Case Studies: Andrew Makin & Val Holmes: Self-Employment in practice

From statistics, it's clear to see that self-employment is growing, yet not everyone who sets out in business does it willingly. Many people prefer a more financially secure way of life and self-employment is a last resort for them. Let's look at two people who are currently working for themselves and see how they view it.

Self-employed subcontractor: Andrew Makin

Andrew, who is qualified and time-served in carpentry and joinery, has worked on a self-employed and sub-contracting basis in the construction industry for over ten years. He stresses that self-employment was not his first choice - he became a sub-contractor when the building companies in North West England changed the way they employed trades people.

The UK Construction Sector is dominated by small firms and demand is location and project based. It is also extremely susceptible to both booms and recessions. When the building companies in Andrew's area began to hire sub-contractors, rather than employing their trades people, self-employment became the only option open to him.

When he set up, he called into his local Tax Office and asked for help and advice. They organised everything for him then and there. Times have changed, and because of the large number of people now entering self-employment, the emphasis is centred more on providing free of charge, short training courses rather than one-to-one help.

At the end of the tax year in April, Andrew pays an accountant to complete his Self Assessment Return. He has recently moved to a firm recommended by colleagues and says it has saved him money because he has paid less tax.

He keeps his payment slips from the building companies, records his business mileage, and keeps any receipts for tools and materials on an on-going basis. Then, at the end of the year, he passes everything onto his accountant who completes the return. This year he paid £250 plus VAT for the service. He knows that other accountants offer lower fees, but he thinks that using someone recommended through word of mouth is better than going for a lower priced option. He has found that a good accountant will ensure you pay the right amount of tax - and only that amount.

Andrew does not think that self-employment is an easy route to take, although he does enjoy the flexibility it allows him. On the downside, his sub-contract work for building companies can finish at a moment's notice and trades people are regularly laid off, especially in the winter months including Christmas and the New Year. He is also personally responsible for buying tools and the cost and running expenses of his van. He does not receive holiday pay or sick pay and has considered taking out private insurance to cover illness, but has found it to be both limiting in what it covers and expensive.

Andrew is one of the many self-employed people in the building sector who have had to get used to self-employment as a way of life because of the fragmentation of the construction industry and the domination of small firms in his local area. In the past there were larger firms offering better jobs in terms of compensation and stability and it has taken some time for many of the skilled tradesmen like him to embrace the challenge that the rising trend towards smaller firms and contracted out services has brought about.

Val Holmes: Business Adviser; Trainer; & Beauty Therapist

Val was employed by a national newspaper group for 25 years and had worked her way up to managing a team of 40 staff across the North of England when she left to start her own business.

With a degree in marketing, she started up on a sole trader basis as a trainer. Initially, she gained a part-time employed lecturing contract with a Further Education College and this allowed her to work at other times as an independent marketing consultant. As she did so, she qualified as a Business Adviser and Mentor and went on to work with government agencies in supporting other start-ups.

All went well until, after a change of government, the funding for the agencies she worked for altered. During that period, work was sporadic, at best. Contracts were sometimes available, but even when they were they had limited timescales. She eventually reached the point where she missed the security of permanent employment and returned to full employment as a media co-ordinator.

Again, her contract ended due to lack of funding. She was asked to stay on and work on a self-employed basis in business development. She agreed to do so, partly because, whilst she had enjoyed working for a regular salary, she had missed the flexibility and variety that self-employment brings. Over the next few months, whilst working with other women who were setting up their own businesses, Val decided to undertake courses in sports massage, holistic therapy, and beauty. It was something she was interested in and when she qualified it would add to the portfolio of services she could offer as a trainer.

She remains self-employed in a variety of roles and now prefers that to employment. She keeps her own books and uses an accountant at year end. It has taken a long time for her to get to where she is and there have been plenty of bumps along the road, but now she has the flexibility and variety she enjoys, and having multiple streams of income has given her the financial peace of mind she needed.

Self-employment is not an easy option as these two case studies show. The good news is that the UK employment rate in January 2017 was the joint highest it's been since comparable records began in 1971. This means there are choices out there – part-time, full-time, or mixed varieties of employment and self-employment – all of which are perfectly acceptable. If you're interested in self-employment, it's a great time to test the market. But first, let's look at how to do it safely and sensibly.

Chapter 3 Book-keeping: Recording business transactions

Once you take money from someone for a sale you've made, you have a potential tax liability.

Potential! The UK tax regime favours start-ups and tariffs are often zero or minimal to begin with, but you must obey the rules of HMRC. This means that, from the EBay trader to the writer, you must record transactions. And it's not that difficult.

Whichever business format you choose, you should record your transactions right from the start. Business expenses are allowable against tax, even at the research stage of setting up a business, plus these records are vital for monitoring the performance of your business.

Organising receipts and bank statements, writing figures into books or inputting them onto spread sheets is for many people the worst aspect of being in business - but without the information (which is in effect feedback on your performance) you have no idea of your business development. Book-keeping records give you pointers on progress as well as the information you need to compile your annual accounts for HRMC.

Start-up expenses

Your record-keeping should start at the idea stage of your business. Make a list any items you buy (from the payment receipts you are given) or any items, such as vehicles, equipment and stock, that you introduce into the business from your own personal property. Find out the current market value for the latter (from E-Bay or some such source). A joiner or a builder, for example, will have his own tools and equipment; similarly hairdressers will have their products and equipment, and consultants and writers will have laptops, stationary and software etc.

Thus, anything you buy, or already own, will be listed along with its cost or market value, together with any cash you introduce. All in all they represent your investment into the business.

Traditionally, an 'Annual Investment Allowance' figure is set in the budget each year. This fixes the capital amount of investment a start-up is allowed to offset against tax in its first year of trading. From January 2016, this became £200,000.

Recording sales income and business expenses

Book-keeping is easy, when you know how. At the simplest level, it is the recording of any money that comes into or goes out of your business.

If you have ever held a car boot sale you will be able to understand how it works. Let's use one as an example:

When you return from the sale you empty your pockets and count the money you have taken. These 'takings' are your sales income - or 'sales revenue' in book-keeping terms. Every day, or at least most days, a business has takings from sales. All you have to do is add up each day's takings and list them on paper or input them onto a computer, noting the date and the amount of money you collected.

It's the same for business expenses. Each day, empty your pockets of all the receipts for items you have purchased and separate those relating to your business. With the car boot sale, you paid an entrance fee, maybe bought a couple of cups of coffee, and then there was the cost of the goods or 'stock' that you sold (you can't include the value of any stock you took but did not sell) and finally, your travel expenses.

For HMRC purposes, it is always better to ask for a receipt when you incur an expense, if you can. A receipt is evidence of payment if ever there is a dispute. However, at a car boot sale it is unlikely that you will be given receipts for all of your purchases. So what do you do?

HMRC should allow any fair and reasonable business expenses to be deducted from your sales income - even those without a receipt - before any tax is calculated. Let's assume you've counted and noted down the takings from the sale – that's the easy bit. Now look at the expenses you incurred.

For a start, you paid an entrance fee (even though you probably weren't given a receipt). That's the first entry under the 'Expenses' heading, set out as follows:

The date

The company organising the event that you paid your entrance fee to

The amount you were charged.

Very straightforward; the remaining expenses are slightly more complicated.

Motor vehicle expenses

With regard to the cost of getting to and from the car boot sale or anywhere else you travel for business purposes, if you take a bus or the train, record the receipt. If you travel in your own vehicle, record the mileage.

Start a 'business mileage log' which you will use at the end of the year to calculate the annual cost of travel. If you are a regular trader and have a vehicle which is used only for business, recording individual journeys is not necessary; the full cost of using the vehicle is a tax deductible expense. However, if you use a vehicle for both personal and business purposes, you keep the mileage log to calculate the split. It's only the business cost of using the vehicle that can be included in your accounts.

A business mileage log is easy to keep, once you get into the habit. Leave a small notebook in your vehicle and jot down the journey details as you go - the date, where you went, and the number of miles. Each mile you travel for business can currently be claimed at 45p per mile for up to 10,000 miles. After that it drops to 25p per mile. It is therefore well worth recording. If your journey to the car boot sale and back was 30 miles, you are able to claim £13.50 (30 x 45p) as a business expense.

Just to explain car mileage further, it is important to realise that HMRC are not going to pay you 45p per business mile. They are going to allow you to offset the cost of your business mileage each year against your takings before they calculate your tax (so you pay less tax). Also, the 45p covers all costs including petrol, car tax, repairs etc.

Subsistence

Let's return to the remainder of the car boot sale expenses - those two cups of coffee and any food you bought; after all you have no receipt for them.

There will always be confusion about expenses such as 'subsistence' and whether or not HMRC will view them as acceptable. The law is that you can claim for 'fair and reasonable' expenses. I was told by an accountant that the tax inspector in my district always looked closely at subsistence and disallowed the high amount of expenses claimed by certain businesses. His view was that people have to eat and drink and that it is only the additional cost (in this case the additional cost of the food and drink above what it would have cost you to make at home) that should be claimed. So, if you are to be fair and reasonable, maybe you could claim 50% of what you paid? Then again, supposing HMRC disagree?

HMRC's treatment of business expenses

When claiming business expenses it's important to remember that the UK Government and its tax representatives want you to start a business. They will not intentionally punish you for minor book-keeping errors - you will not be sent to prison if you make a mistake, although you will be if you are consistently and deliberately dishonest.

If you include in your accounts any business expenses that HMRC disapprove of, they might surcharge you with the amount of tax you avoided by claiming them. You have the right to appeal and it is what would be deemed fair and reasonable in a Court of Law that counts. Don't be afraid to claim expenses that you feel are justifiable – it's obviously better to check first if you're unsure. HMRC run workshops on a variety of topics, including business expenses. Look at their website for information if you are unsure about an item.

Stock

The final expense of the car boot sale is the cost of stock - the price you paid for the goods you sold there, or the present-day value of anything you own that you sold.

If you purchased stock specifically to sell at the car boot sale you will probably have receipts for it. If the goods were your own, then you have to value them at market price. Either way, the amount will be entered on the list of expenses as stock, with the appropriate cost price or value.

Summarising business transactions

So that's it; job done, book-keeping completed as below:

Sales - £250.00

Expenses:

Travel (30miles @ 45p) - £13.50

Entrance Fee - £10.00

Subsistence - £2.00

Stock - £100.00

Calculating profit

By regularly recording your income and expenses you will be fulfilling your legal requirements and keeping a record which, at the end of the tax year, will give you the 3 magic figures for your Self-Assessment Return:

Sales - £250.00

Expenses - £125.50

Profit - £124.50

Many traders are blasé about record keeping. They say things like, 'I know I'm doing okay because I sold a load of stuff at the car boot sale for £250 and only paid £100 for it. I don't need to write it down, I know what to buy and I'm good at selling it.'

With records, you can see that the profit was only £124.50 not £150.00 - not much of a difference, but if you did this with all of your transactions you would have an inflated idea of your profit and less to claim against tax.

Debtors and Creditors

Non-cash businesses - often service providers - regularly have money owing to them by customers. These customers are known as debtors. Similarly, there may be suppliers and providers of services who the business owes money to - these people are your creditors.

When you send out invoices and are not paid immediately (because you've allowed the customer credit) you should keep a list of the invoices and mark them off with the payment date when they are settled. It's the same for invoices from your creditors too.

This system is known as 'credit control'. From the outstanding balances on your lists, you will know who to chase up for money owing and who you need to pay. It will give you a clearer picture of the true financial position of the business.

Cash and bank balances

A constant running total of all money transactions, both in cash and through the business bank account, should be maintained right from the outset. It is very easy to become overdrawn and, if you do, you will incur expensive bank charges. There is also the fact that small cash transactions in or out of the business mount up over time. If they are unrecorded they will not be claimed against your taxes and you will pay more than necessary.

Online banking makes it easy to check your account daily. This should become routine; it is far too common for new businesses to become overdrawn. Late payments from customers and unexpected or unplanned expenses often send business bank accounts into the red and incur high charges. (One of the benefits of choosing a business banking service with dedicated managers who are accessible and supportive is that if it looks as though there are going to be problems with your account, you can call and ask for advice.)

If you do not use online banking, keep a written record showing the bank balance at the start of the day, adjusted for the ins and outs and giving you a closing balance. This type of record can be used for cash transactions too.

Book-keeping systems

If all you do is write down all of your business incomings and out-goings, file the receipts and keep your mileage log, you will cover the essentials necessary to run a book-keeping system in the early stages of your business.

Spread-sheets & Computerised Accounts Packages

Excel spread sheets are very popular with start-ups. They take away the pain of manual book-keeping and allow you to use formulae for the calculations. Setting up a separate sheet for sales takings and another for business expenses (date - who you paid - amount) will get you started. A list of debtors and creditors is also easy to set up and

maintain on Excel.

There are computerised account packages (such as Sage, Xero and QuickBooks) which are brilliant, but if you are not familiar with them it will take you a while - and a fair amount of frustration - to learn how to use them. You need to ask yourself if learning an accounts package is the best use of your time at the start of your business. Use a simple system that suits you and focus on your business in the early days.

Book-keeping has many benefits and should become a habit. It will help you to cost out jobs or projects, provide customers with value for money yet profitable quotes, and help you set your selling prices. It also acts as a great guide in showing you which areas of your business are profitable and which need attention. This keeps you moving forward and gives you the stability to grow.

If you really do not want to do your own book-keeping, then get someone to do it for you. Arrange regular meetings with them, though - you must know what's going on in your business and the figures are there to guide you. If you understand them you will be able to ask the right questions that help you move forward.

Chapter 4 Raising finance & Business Banking

Accessing finance as a start-up business

When considering a business idea, people naturally think about how much it will cost them to get started. Whilst the government have set up small loans funds for start-up businesses (usually accessed through the Enterprise Agencies) more and more people are bootstrapping – borrowing as little money as possible at the outset. So which is best – borrowing or bootstrapping?

Loans have to be repaid – with interest. The conditions attached to the loans are sometimes complex and there can be hidden costs on top of the interest, such as early repayment penalties and administration fees. Once you have committed to a loan, the repayments become fixed costs - they have to be repaid even if your business doesn't get off the ground. This is what the advocates of bootstrapping want you to realise; they recommend starting out without incurring future debt wherever possible.

Obviously not all start-ups can manage without borrowing and some purposely choose to borrow.

Government agencies and the major banks are the safest lenders to borrow from initially.

Before you start, make a list of what you need to get your business idea off the ground – don't forget that this is often idealistic; view it as a starting point. Such lists tend to include a van or motor vehicle, premises to operate from, equipment to work with, and cash to buy stock and pay for any expenses. If you cost out your ideal start-up list, you will probably find it impossible to finance; most lists have to be pared down to the essentials.

It is possible to start-up with a small amount of money – like the £100 Lord Sugar gives candidates on 'The Apprentice'. They go out and buy stock, find what sells, and go back with the profits to buy more of it. Using your sales income to finance the business is what it's about, but to survive for any length of time you need regular customers and cash reserves for when there is a lull in sales.

For start-up businesses, in the beginning sales income will be slow and sporadic and there will still be expenses to pay for - even if it is only petrol for your car or bus or rail tickets. This means that if you do not have any money of your own, or family and friends to support you by giving or lending you money, you will probably have to borrow elsewhere - if not at the beginning of your business start-up, maybe at some later time when your sales take off.

Where do you go for finance?

If you need to borrow money because you lack personal savings or friends or family to help you out, your first enquiries should be made to the Government Agencies.

Finance for start-ups is difficult to come by and often expensive because of their high risk of failure. Enterprise Agencies and other organisations such as the Job Centres are government-funded to help people start out in business. As mentioned in the introduction, they often help by giving advice and providing training in business skills - particularly in developing a business plan. As the evidence supports the view that start-ups with business plans are significantly more likely to survive, the government will only offer grants or loans to start-ups with a viable business plan.

If there are no available grants or loans, many start-ups will approach a bank for finance.

Banks offer finance in the form of loans, overdrafts, credit cards...... all of which can help with cash flow. Start-ups without a track record might struggle to meet a bank's lending criteria, though, especially if the owner has a poor credit history. If your lending application isn't initially accepted by a bank, don't give up. There are many banks trying to attract start-up businesses. Search online as well as visiting those in your local area, always bearing in mind that at that moment in time your business may not be considered ready to take on finance.

Business Plans

Any potential lender will want to see a plan of what you are going to use their money for. Your business plan will be checked against the lender's specific criteria and they will assess the likelihood of you repaying their loan.

They will also require some form of security from you, just in case the business does not go as planned. They tend to fix the interest rate at a level in accordance with their perceived risk - the higher they view the risk of the business failing, the higher the rate of interest charged.

Agencies and the banks all have to feel confident that the business will repay the loan and any interest on it. A sound business plan is the key to offering them this reassurance.

How do you start up if you can't borrow any money?

This is what bootstrapping is about. You test your business idea in whatever way you can and with whatever resources you are able to get your hands on, like in The Apprentice. If you can show from this that there is a market for your business proposition, and that it's likely to be successful, a finance provider will look more favourably at your requirements. As mentioned earlier, often people can't get the finance to start-up in their ideal way – they make do until they have a proven track record and then approach the lenders.

When you are considering and costing out a business idea, at some point you will be faced with a 'reality check' – a point at which you have to weigh it up realistically and make a decision as to the financial viability of your idea. This is the time to assess the situation, look at the information you have gathered and ask yourself if you really want to attempt a start-up.

There is always a way of starting a business on a shoestring. For traders, if you can manage initially without buying a van, or leasing premises, or buying such a high level of stock, why not test your idea on, say, a market stall or E-Bay? In that way you will develop a business history showing demand and if you approach a lender with a plan based on facts and figures, they are likely to look more favourably at your proposition – particularly if you have orders in the pipeline and have taken advice and attended business courses to develop your enterprise skills.

Business Bank Accounts

One of the questions people ask when setting up a business is, 'Do I need a business bank account?'

Legally, you do not have to have a business bank account. Practically, it is better to have a business bank account, for the following reasons:

A business bank account will create a history of transactions which develop into a credit rating. A good credit rating makes raising finance for your business in the form of loans and overdrafts easier.

A separate bank account for your business transactions makes maintaining your book-keeping records simpler and tidier. Everything is in one account and you can use the statements as evidence of incomings and outgoings for tax purposes, particularly if you do not have receipts.

Because of money laundering regulations, bank employees look closely at accounts which have a lot of cash transactions. If they think you are running a business through a personal account, a bank can close it and insist you open a business one.

A business bank account gives your start-up credibility. Your potential customers will see it as a legitimate undertaking and this will offset some of the risk they might feel in dealing with a new business.

How do I open a business bank account and how much will it cost me?

Like many things, the world of business banking is changing. If you have a personal bank account that you've kept in good order, the logical place to start your search for a business bank account is with that bank. Word of mouth recommendation is also valuable, especially from people with a business similar to yours.

The internet is the best place to look for price comparison information. In the past, anyone setting up a new business would have to choose between a high street bank and a private bank, often online-only. The benefit of a high street bank such as Barclays or HSBC was that there were local branches with specialist managers available to help with business planning. Personal managers are diminishing and there are now a vast number of options on the online front – banks that give you access to state-of-the-art money management apps.

At the time of writing, Barclays, Lloyds and HSBC all offer between 6 and 18 months free banking. After that there is an annual account fee of £60 - £78. Then there are varying charges for transactions. It's complicated - before you even know if you'll be accepted - but you have to start somewhere. And once you have a business banking history, it gets easier. Then you can switch providers if you wish.

Businesses that deal predominately with cash transactions are the hardest hit when it comes to charges. The days of counting and bagging money at the counter are disappearing; they're being priced out. Depositing cash at the counter currently incurs fees, whilst most electronic transactions are free.

In Summary

In reality, many start-ups and established businesses undergo difficulties with cash flow. When receipts of money due to them are paid late, it can result in a shortage of funds and any subsequent bank direct debits and standing order payments might be declined and bank charges applied.

If you can find a bank with dedicated business managers, it will avoid making time-consuming phone calls to call centres if you hit a problem.

Before you start up, research what's available. After one year you will have an established track record and most banks will try to retain you as a client. Further facilities such as overdrafts and loans, which are difficult to attain at the outset, will become available to you as a result of proving that you can organise your business transactions effectively.

Prior to the next chapters which relate to the financial sections of business plans, let's take a look at a business which started over twenty years ago. Let's see how Christine Anne Rowland's Beauty & Holistic Therapy business (now Esme Beauty & Skin Therapy) dealt with everything we've discussed so far.

Case Study Part 1: Christine Anne Rowlands: Beauty & Holistic Therapy

Christine started her business in the 1990's with the help of her local Enterprise Agency. She qualified in holistic therapy and then worked for two years in an established beauty salon where she practised her profession and added to her skills. Whilst employed, she gained experience in how a successful salon was run and this was invaluable when she opened hers. Encouraged by her family, she decided to test the market by renting a room in her sister's business premises. From there she opened her own salon which continues to flourish.

Start-up Help

Whilst she was researching her business idea, Christine found that there were grants of £1,000 available to start-ups in her local area. The grant was subject to the approval of a viable business plan and training and one-to-one advice was available to assist the applicant with this. Further advice and monitoring for the first year of the business was also accessible.

She approached her local Enterprise Agency,

attended the business start-up workshops, and was then allocated a Business Adviser. He worked with her on a one-to-one basis, helping her to complete a business plan. Christine says that she had excellent help in setting up her business and recommends that start-ups explore all avenues of current business support. Later, when she expanded her business, she had to re-write her business plan and found that her Local Authority was also helpful in providing advice and support.

She set up as a sole trader and has remained one - even though her business has grown, she has moved to her own premises, and has two employees.

Initially she found the financial aspects of the business daunting and admits that she would have struggled to write a business plan without considerable help from both her adviser and her husband. Christine's daughter set her up with a simple book-keeping system which consisted of two daily lists, the first one for her takings and the second one for business expenses. These records were hand-written and filed in a folder, along with the receipts relating to them. Christine is very meticulous; in fact her Business Adviser told her that she kept her records better than he kept his.

Since she set up she has used two different

accountants. Whilst the first one was excellent in terms of completing her Self Assessment Return, as the business grew she found she needed help with other aspects of the business such as employee wages, tax and National Insurance and the other legal aspects of employing people.

Whilst she still keeps her lists, her daughter now completes the book-keeping on a computerised accounting system which the accountant recommended. This can be easily converted to what he requires at year end. Christine has not found his cost to be prohibitive, but she is aware that without the help of her daughter on the book-keeping side, it would be a lot more expensive.

With regard to registering for VAT, Christine was happy for her sales to remain below the VAT threshold until she was confident that she could run the business. She knows this is not an option for all businesses, for example, those selling cars and barges (her examples - not sure where the barges came from....) but it made it less complicated for her.

When it came to financing the business, Christine says that because of her maturity and the fact that she had been employed for a long period of time, she had savings and did not need external borrowing. She also had the benefit of the government grant (unfortunately these have all but disappeared and been replaced by loans). She had the choice of borrowing and scaling up at the outset, but she chose to rent a room in her sister-in-law's premises in order to keep her start-up expenses and running costs low until she knew the business was successful and sustainable.

To begin with, she opened a business bank account which offered her 18 months free banking. When the business grew and her banking requirements changed – she was depositing significant amounts of cash for which there was a charge and taking card payments that also incurred a cost - she asked other business people who came into the salon which bank they used and listened to their recommendations. Then she telephoned around and found that better terms were available from a competitor. She recommends that start-up businesses do the same - work it out as you go along, especially by talking to other people who are in business.

Business Plans

Christine had to write a business plan when she applied for the grant. She says that it made her familiar with aspects of business she would otherwise be ignorant of - especially the legal aspects. When I asked her about Health & Safety (H&S) requirements, she said she just knew about them and then realised that this was because, at every stage of her training, H&S had been included – when studying for her holistic therapy qualification and when she undertook the start-up business training.

Work experience had also given her an insight into the practical aspects of H&S and other legal obligations. Later, when her business grew and she moved to larger premises, she had to re-think her legal requirements and produce another business plan in order to obtain the relevant planning permission and change of use authorisation.

Christine says that there is plenty of support out there for the small business and that it is invaluable. We'll look at her business again when we come to the other legal aspects of starting a business.

Chapter 5 Forecasting Sales

The majority of people with a business idea just want to get out there and start. If they discover that they need a business plan, particularly to obtain funding, many of them see this as an obstacle.

Statistics show that start-ups with business plans have double the chance success – that's why government agencies and the banks insist on them.

They always offer help and support and the outcome is worthwhile. It's far easier to make decisions if the facts and figures are set out before you - this is what a business plan does. You forecast your sales figures and expenses month by month. This highlights any seasonal fluctuations and when you've finished you will have a good idea as to whether your business venture is financially viable. If the plan shows that, after buying stock and paying for any business expenses, there is enough money left over for taxes and your living costs, you will start off confidently.

You do not want to undertake all the hard work that a start-up involves and find at the end of the year that you have little or nothing to show for it. A surprising number of people take on leases for premises on a whim and without any financial knowledge or skills. Many spend long, and often boring, hours in an outlet that has very few customers, worrying about how they are going to pay their rent and expenses and repay their loans. By gaining a little financial know-how, you can avoid this.

Writing a Business Plan

Your business plan is the story of your business. It is a great motivator because it's a way of setting goals.

You now realise that if you are looking to borrow money or receive any form of grant, the finance provider will want to see a business plan. Also, as they are in effect your financiers, you will need to write the plan their way.

When your business plan is submitted for approval, a Bank Manager or a Business Adviser will spend probably less than half an hour on reading it and assessing the information. Then they will make a decision as to whether or not to grant or lend you money. Because they have limited time to study your proposal, business plans have a format. They are laid out in a way that makes it easy for the reader to evaluate the business proposition. Most lenders will expect you to use their specific format – they will usually give you a template showing how to set out the sections – and it is not difficult, once you have understood the jargon and prepared the information they require.

Personal information, your profile or CV, a sales and marketing strategy, and financial projections for the first year of the business are all outlined in a business plan. This book deals with the financial and legal aspects of a business start-up and it is the following areas that we shall focus on:

The Sales Forecast

The Profit & Loss (P&L) Forecast

The Cash Flow Forecast (CFF)

The Balance Sheet

The Sales Forecast

The starting point of the financial projections is generally the sales forecast – although business start-ups that are acquiring premises and taking on debt may complete the expenses forecast first. We'll look at that later.

A lender will expect you to estimate, or predict, your sales income on a month-by-month basis for at least the first 12 months. This will then give you your annual sales figure (also known as the sales turnover).

The reason lenders want to see the information month by month is because it demonstrates the highs-and-lows that all businesses experience and is a means of planning around cash fluctuations. By understanding these variances, often arising because of your customers' buying habits, you will be able to assess when to buy in stock, when to adjust your prices through promotions and discounts, when to get in extra labour.......and so forth.

Each business will be subject to market trends and seasonal variations. By showing that you have looked at economic statistics and studied your market by researching similar businesses, a lender will look more favourably on your projections.

When we ask people in business planning workshops to come up with their sales projections, they are often horrified, having no idea of how or where to start.

Where to start: Selling prices

The easiest way to start a sales forecast is to set your selling prices. Selling prices should always be fixed in line with those of your closest competitor. Your selling prices will be made up of individual prices for products, or an hourly, daily, weekly or contract rate if you are offering a service.

The rule for setting selling prices is to base them on what the market will bear or the going rate. This means they should be set at what your particular customers are willing to pay (and this is generally in line with what your local competitors are charging).

Once you come up with your selling prices, you then need to estimate how many customers you will have each month and the quantity of products and services they will buy from you.

Let's look at different businesses and see how the owners estimate their monthly sales figures.

Competitors' selling prices

Finding out about your competitors, including their selling prices, is a major part of market research. As well as discovering what they charge, you should also look at how they run their businesses. To compete successfully you need to know both their prices and what they're offering, and then at least match it. If you can improve on it, that will give you a competitive advantage.

A plumber, a joiner, a builder, or a business trainer will set an hourly, daily and weekly rate, and be able to quote for contract work. Where a business sells products, it is detailed and time consuming work. You will need to list individual products and mark them up to your selling price, then check those prices against those of your competitors.

Once this is done, you will then estimate the number of customers each month and the quantity they will buy from you.

For services, decide how many working days are available to you each month, or how many days you will be open for business. Each month will vary – use a business diary for planning.

As an aside, a business diary is a valuable tool because you can jot down in one place details such as vehicle mileage, money you've taken from customers or paid out to suppliers etc.....and use it later to update your book-keeping system.

Next, you must attempt to predict the number of workdays you are likely to obtain work for – not that easy, be conservative in your estimates; it's in your best interest to be realistic.

Where you have an outlet such as a shop, café, bar or restaurant, you can simplify your forecast by estimating the likely average spend per customer rather than costing out each item sold. If you can find a set of accounts for a similar business – maybe one that's currently on the market for sale – they should give you some indication of a typical year's sales. You will still have to break the figure down month by month though.

It's worth repeating that if you are borrowing finance for your business, the more detail on selling prices and potential customers that you can research, the more likely is it that your lending application will be successful. A bank manager or business adviser will be aware of the typical sales for a business such as yours and will look closely at your forecast and ask how you came up with your projections.

To summarise; your monthly sales figures will be forecast by:

For a service - the hourly, daily or contract rate you charge, multiplied by the estimated number of working hours or days each month.

For products – sales figures based on the number of customers each month multiplied by their average spend– for example, 50 customers spending on average £5 each.

Formatting the Sales Forecast

To set out a sales forecast, draw 13 columns on a piece of paper and, starting with the month you commence trading, label each one with the following months and end with a total column. Beneath each heading, write down the value of sales in £'s. Add up the 12 months' figures and this becomes your predicted sales turnover for the year.

Seasonal Variations

No business has the same number of sales for each month of the year and a lender knows this. Monthly or seasonal sales variations are common to all businesses. For example, January is a month of low sales for many businesses as potential customers are cash-poor after the Christmas period. There are exceptions such as gym memberships and exercise and slimming programmes, but generally speaking, businesses are likely to experience a slump in sales.

Good businesses know when they will be busy and stock up accordingly. In periods of downturn, they offer discounts and run sales promotions in order to retain their existing customers and to attract new ones.

Once your forecast is complete, you will be aware of the ups and downs in sales and can move on to estimating your business expenses. You'll be pleased to know that this is much easier.

Chapter 6 Profit & Loss

Forecasting business expenses

Forecasting your monthly business expenses is easier and more accurate than forecasting sales. For example, a letting agent will provide you with the costs of leases for premises and the rent, rates, and service charges they incur. Similarly stockists, providers of equipment, accountants, banks and legal firms will all give you quotes for their services.

Personal Survival Budget

Finance providers like to see a Personal Survival Budget – a statement of the owner's personal monthly incomings and outgoings. When they compare this to your business forecasts they can see if you will be able to survive financially (and be able to repay their debt).

There is a term for money taken out of a business by owners for their own use; it is 'drawings'. The drawings from your business should be enough to provide you with the income you need to live on - as shown in your Personal Survival Budget - although they may be supplemented by other income from full or part-time employed work, pensions or benefits, and so forth.

Fixed Costs

If your business is a mobile one, or if you are working from home, your business expenses will be less than those of a business with fixed costs such as rent and service charges.

Fixed costs are amounts of money that have to be paid out each month - irrespective of customer sales. They include rent, rates, wages, and loan repayments.

If your business has fixed costs, you need to consider your expenses and estimate what you need in sales income to cover them and your taxes – and make a wage for yourself.

Any fixed costs should be seriously thought about at start-up. When you borrow money there will be regular loan and interest repayments to meet. When you acquire premises there will be the monthly rent and service costs, right from the outset. Then, if you decide to employ someone, there will be regular wage payments and benefits to provide for. All of these expenses occur before you have time to establish a regular customer base and they create a cash time-lag. Without an initial outlay of cash, you will struggle to meet your financial obligations.

Finance providers look carefully at the fixed costs included in a business plan. They will ask you to justify your forecasted sales figures, especially those in the early months, and look at your cash injection to see if it is sufficient for survival. When you know that over 20% of businesses fail in their first year, this is hardly surprising.

Break-even Analysis

This calculation shows the point at which a business is making enough profit from sales to cover its fixed costs. It is a measure used by the banks and other lenders when analysing a business plan.

Calculating the Break-even point

Break-even is difficult to understand, let alone calculate, for many start-ups. The simplest way of explaining it is to take a mobile business (no fixed costs) and compare it to one with rented premises (a fixed cost).

A start-up mobile hairdresser, for example, will buy products and incur transport costs - only when they have a customer. The hairdresser who rents a room or a chair in a salon has to pay a landlord – irrespective of whether they have customers or not.

With no fixed costs, even if the mobile business's sales forecast proves to have been over-optimistic, it does not affect their cash position adversely. For the hairdresser who is renting space, it does because they have to meet their rent payments even if they do not work.

Taking this a step further, let's assume the average selling price for a hair treatment is £40, of which £10 is profit for the hairdresser. It will take five sales to cover the cost of a £50 rental liability. That is the point at which they break even. It's only after those five sales that they start to make a profit.

Break-even analysis is particularly important if profit is low and fixed costs are high, for example, restaurants and public houses. Because sales demand has to start off and remain high, leisure and hospitality businesses are viewed as higher risk ventures and break-even analysis is a crucial element in predicting their success or failure. The banks and other lenders need assurances that there will be enough customers to cover the costs and make a profit before they will lend.

Profit Margins

Another concept financiers are interested in is the profit margin. This is a measure used by trading businesses (those buying and selling goods) to monitor performance.

For example, if you sell an item on E-bay for £10 and it costs you £5, you make a Gross Profit (the profit before you pay out any expenses such as advertising or postage) of £5.

This can be displayed as follows:

Sales £10
Cost of Sales £5
Gross Profit £5

In the case of a trading business, finance providers calculate the Gross Profit figure as a percentage – the margin.

To do this they divide it (£5) by the sales figure (£10) and multiply the result by 100 – in this case the result is a 50% profit margin.

Measuring profit margin is important for businesses that manufacture or sell products - it indicates how efficiently you buy and sell your stock. When your manufacturing or product cost prices rise, your profit margins fall. When you lower your costs or increase your selling prices, it raises the profit margin.

Selling Services: Indirect Costs or Overheads

Where people sell services rather than products there are often no direct costs or profit margins to manage. For example, a financial adviser or a book-keeper is unlikely to have any *direct* costs - unless they buy and sell stock as well as provide services. They will have *indirect* costs – travel, stationery, computers etc. – but these are simply business expenses (also referred to as overheads).

Business plans for service providers are less complicated because there is no Gross Profit calculation. Expenses are listed and then deducted from the sales forecast to give an overall Net Profit figure. However, service providers still have to be aware of any fixed costs. As with traders, these have to be met whether they have customers or not.

Formatting the Profit & Loss Forecast

Once you have estimated your annual business expenses and broken them down into monthly fixed or variable costs, you are ready to complete your Profit & Loss forecast. Again, set out thirteen columns, one for each month and an annual total.

For traders, the sales forecast prepared earlier is the top line of the P&L Forecast. This is followed by the Cost of Sales - the cost of stock you buy each month to fulfil your sales.

When you deduct your cost of stock from your sales, you have the Gross Profit. This is the amount you will make from trading – simply buying and selling products.

Your forecast expenses are then detailed line by line into categories appropriate to your business – for example, rent, rates, services, wages, administration, motor vehicle and so on..... Then they are totalled and deducted from the Gross Profit to give you the Net Profit (also known as the bottom line).

For businesses selling services, there is no Gross Profit calculation. You simply transfer your forecast sales and deduct the forecast expenses, leaving you with the Net Profit.

Reality check

These financial projections allow you to consider the viability of your business proposition. The Net Profit is the amount of money you will end up with each month, before you take any drawings and set aside money for taxes. This is when a Personal Survival Budget is invaluable. You know how much you need to live on and you've predicted the business return by way of profit through your financial forecasts.

Let's return to Christine Anne Rowlands and look at how she weighed up the financial situation when she considered moving from a rented room to leasing larger and substantially more expensive business premises.

Case Study Part 2: Christine Anne Rowlands Holistic and Beauty Therapy

As Christine's client base grew, she reached the stage where she had outgrown her rented room and had to decide about the future of her business. To grow or standstill is the predicament that many businesses find themselves in once they become established.

As well as outgrowing the space, clients were asking Christine for additional beauty treatments such as nail extensions that she was unable to deliver.

At this time, residential premises further along the road became available and she enquired about leasing them. They were formerly residential premises, as opposed to business premises, and although the landlord was keen for her to rent them, it meant she would have to obtain planning permission from her Local Authority for a change of use. On contacting the Town Hall she was told that the officers responsible would need to see a revised business plan before permission could be considered.

At this stage uncertainty crept in. Christine knew this was a far reaching business decision and that she needed another view and additional support before undertaking the move. She recommends acquiring advice from reliable and knowledgeable sources at each development stage in your business. In her case, she sought advice from the local authority and then sat down with her husband to calculate the cost of the move and the revised monthly on-going expenses. They added a further 20% to the expenses to act as a safety net if they had underestimated.

Once the expenses were forecast, it was easy for Christine to calculate how many additional client sales she would need to cover the extra costs as she knew the average spend per customer by then.

As she looked for ways of trimming the expenses and expanding her services, she decided to let one of the rooms in the new premises to a nail technician. This meant that she would be able to offer the treatment her customers most frequently requested and that the income from sub-letting would also contribute to her additional expenses - she was taking on two floors of a building and there was an extra room already available.

After more discussion and consideration she decided that the nail technician would have to be self-employed. Taking on an employee at a time when she was already undertaking a step-change would be too much of a financial and legal commitment for her.

Christine would have loved to have walked straight into her new premises without all of this detailed consideration. Her business is her passion and although she had started out well, she knew she had to expand in a controlled way. By revising her Sales and Profit & Loss Forecasts, she was able to see exactly how many new customers, or increased sales to existing customers, she had make to stay afloat financially. She persevered with all of the detailed scheduling. She did not particularly enjoy it, but knew that once her business plan was revised she could get back to what she enjoyed - focusing on her clients and their treatments.

A profitable business cannot survive without sufficient capital and cash to keep it going over time. This is why, once you have created a Profit & Loss Forecast, potential investors expect you to convert it into a Cash Flow Forecast. That's what we'll look at in the next chapter.

Chapter 7: Cash Flow Forecasting

Cash is King!

A Profit & Loss Forecast gives you an insight into how your business is likely to perform and, as we have seen, the better the research, the more realistic the forecast will be.

But being profitable in business is not enough. If you run out of cash before you start to make a profit, you will be unable to trade. Because of this, lenders are more interested in a Cash Flow Forecast than in a P&L Forecast.

How is the Cash Flow Forecast (CFF) different from the P&L Forecast?

A Cash Flow Forecast is different from a P & L Forecast because it shows, month by month, how the money flows into and out of your business.

To begin with your expenses are likely to be higher than your sales income. This means you must have a sufficient backdrop of cash (or credit) to keep your business flowing along.

Cash flow is particularly difficult for businesses that offer *credit* terms to their customers - where, for example, you allow your customers to take products or services and pay at a later date. Most business expenses have to be paid as they occur; some might have to be paid in advance, like rent. Whilst you are waiting for customers to come on board, or for the income from credit sales you've made, your cash will be depleting.

In a Profit & Loss Forecast, sales are recorded in the month they are made - not when they are paid for. Thus the statement is useful for budgeting purposes, but it does not show the true cash position of the business.

A Cash Flow Forecast highlights delayed sales income and identifies where this will result in negative cash flow (when expenses exceed sales income).

Businesses all have cash flow fluctuations – especially at the start. Even businesses that don't offer credit terms will have to wait for cash from late-paying customers. When you send out an invoice for goods or services that the customer has agreed to pay within a certain timeframe, there's no guarantee that they will.

As a start-up business, sadly, there is little you can do about late-paying customers. You can complain and threaten to take legal action, but it's expensive and time-consuming and there are always competitors who your customer may choose to use instead of you. Once you become established you will have more power, but at start-up you are likely to be held to their terms and conditions rather than yours.

For all of these reasons, lenders will always prefer to see a Cash Flow Forecast rather than a Profit & Loss Forecast.

Working Capital

Working capital is the cash you hold to provide for the fluctuations and imbalances in receipts and payments on a day- to- day basis. A lack of it is one of the main reasons businesses fail early on.

It's already been stressed that whilst you are waiting for receipts of money from customers, you have to carry on making payments for stock and your business expenses and this is why you must remain cash positive.

A Cash Flow Forecast will show you when your outgoings are at their highest in comparison with your incomings and will enable you to organise corrective action - credit facilities like a bank overdraft or a credit card in order to tide yourself over in the short-term.

Christine Anne Rowlands experienced cash flow problems when she moved to her own premises - even though she had carefully researched and revised her business plan. She found she had failed to take everything into account.

From the start, Christine made the decision to use high quality, branded products for her treatments. They were expensive and, as a new customer, the product manufacturers were unwilling to offer her credit terms. They expected to be paid up-front on a 'pro-forma invoice' basis – immediate payment on receipt of the goods - and order a certain level of stock, varying from 500 to 1000 units (sometimes the minimum order was quoted in £'s rather than units of stock). With regard to nail products, the main supplier had a £450 minimum initial order price. Other suppliers accepted smaller orders, but all of them insisted on payment up-front.

These costs had been missed on her revised business plan and if she had not set aside the 20% safety net figure, she would have been unable to afford the stock for her new range of treatments.

In conclusion, a Profit & Loss Forecast is a valuable tool because it shows you if your business will be profitable, but by converting it into a Cash Flow Forecast it becomes far more useful in preventing cash deficiencies that can halt or closedown a business.

Always remember that profitable businesses will fail without adequate cash flow.

Chapter 8 Balance Sheets

The Balance Sheet was once considered an integral part of any business plan but less emphasis is placed on it for today's start-ups. The main areas of focus are now seen as sales generation, profitability, and cash flow.

Understanding a Balance Sheet makes a positive difference to serious business people. It impacts on how they invest in their business, grow it, and re-invest to create their own personal wealth.

What is a Balance Sheet?

A Balance Sheet is a statement of assets (what a business owns) and liabilities (what it owes) at any given point in time.

The difference between the assets and the liabilities represents the owner's capital investment – their stake in the business.

Watching your capital investment increase as you work hard in a business is motivating. It encourages owners to minimise their drawings and re-invest so that liabilities are reduced, assets are added to, and the business worth increases.

Put simply, a Balance Sheet shows the value and the state of the financial affairs of a business at any given date.

Growing your Balance Sheet

Growing your Balance Sheet is the way to increase your wealth - to get rich. You'll probably have very little in the way of assets at start-up, but as your business increases its assets – its stock and cash, for example – and reduces its credit and loans, the Balance Sheet tips to the positive side.

By using your profit to grow your Balance Sheet you will add to the value of the business, increase its wealth and stability, and your investment.

Balance Sheet divisions

In a formal Balance Sheet, the assets and liabilities are separated into the following categories:

Fixed Assets - these are long-term items with a lifetime of longer than 1 year, for example, buildings and equipment.

Current Assets –these are short-term items with a lifetime of less than 1 year, for example, debtors and cash.

Long Term Liabilities - debts with a lifetime of longer than 1 year, for example, mortgages and the capital the business owes to its owner.

Current Liabilities – these are short-term debts with a lifetime of less than one year, for example, creditors and bank overdrafts (short-term because they can be called in at any time).

Liquidity

The reason assets and liabilities are allocated time periods is because it shows the liquidity of a business – the ease with which the current assets can be converted into cash to pay off the liabilities.

Cash flow is the lifeblood of a business. If for any reason the sales income dries up, if everything is invested into long-term assets such as property or investments, the owner will struggle to meet any payments due. Fixed assets cannot immediately be turned into cash and will not solve the problem.

A Balance Sheet identifies immediate liabilities and provides information as to the level of short-term assets, particularly cash, which covers them. Whilst a business might invest well, it needs immediate cash to pay its creditors. It's a balancing act.

Over time, lenders will want to look at a Balance Sheet to see its current position in terms of both investment and solvency. For start-ups it has less relevance - the assets and liabilities are generally smaller. Nevertheless, if you can master your understanding of the Balance Sheet, it is of great use in managing and growing the financial strength of your business.

Chapter 9: Other legal aspects of business

It will be clear by now that working for yourself or starting a business involves far more personal responsibility than working for an employer. You alone are responsible for everything. If your business grows and you employ others, you will then have a responsibility for them too. You will have to calculate and deduct their taxes and National Insurance (as well as your own) and send the money to HMRC, plus you will have legal responsibilities such as their Health & Safety to consider. Whilst this might seem overwhelming, it is not impossible. In this chapter, we'll look at the main areas of the law that start-up businesses need to be familiar with.

Business Insurances

Anyone who works for themselves can be sued. They have legal responsibilities under the law - including adhering to Health & Safety regulations and meeting the requirements of Trading Standards - and can be taken to court if they fail to comply with any of the regulations relating to their business.

For example, a business selling food could be sued if a customer suffers an illness and claims it was a result of eating a product they bought from them. Solicitors, accountants and financial advisers can be sued for giving wrongful advice. Tradesmen are similarly liable if their work is faulty.

As a business person you are always open to complaints and disputes can lead to legal action against you – even when it's not your fault. Because of this, you must have the appropriate business insurances in place. You might never need to use them, but you have to protect yourself and the business against claims.

Business insurance falls into two categories:

Professional Indemnity Insurance - insurance cover for those offering professional services.

Public Liability (including product liability) – is insurance for businesses in direct contact with the general public.

Where do people find business insurance?

Banks, Brokers, Professional or Trade Associations and a variety of internet companies sell insurance.

If you use your bank, a broker or a trade association to purchase business insurance, the person dealing with you should be able to offer specific advice as to which insurance best meets your needs. If you buy it on the internet, you will have to study the specifications and ensure they cover all eventualities in relation to your business. It makes sense to use a specialist rather than finding the cheapest deal on a website, even if it costs more. It can save you time and money in the long term.

Business insurance is often not as expensive as start-ups expect. For many, it ranges from around £100 to £250 per year and can usually be paid for in instalments. For higher risk businesses, such as scaffolding firms (where claims are likely to be expensive) the cost will be substantially higher.

Notifying your personal insurance providers and other interested parties

As well as looking at business insurance, you should look at your own insurances - your home and motor vehicle policies – and check that they cover you for working from home or on a self-employed basis.

If you fail to tell your existing providers that you are using your home and vehicle for business purposes and later have a claim made against you, they are unlikely to pay out. Reputable insurance companies will not overcharge you for your change in circumstances unless there is significantly increased risk. There might be additional conditions, for example when a tradesman leaves tools or equipment in a vehicle overnight. Most insurance conversions do not carry a surcharge and if there is a small additional premium to pay, it's always worthwhile.

As well as your house and vehicle insurance, when you work from home you are legally obliged to notify your mortgage provider or landlord and the local authority that collects your council tax. Again, additional premiums or business rates will only be applied in exceptional circumstances. Each provider will have their own terms and conditions and for many start-ups there will be no extra cost.

Health & Safety (H&S) Legislation

Health & Safety legislation applies to anyone who works for themselves - you can be taken to court if you do not comply with it.

There will be certain aspects of H&S legislation which relate specifically to your type of business. The government website www.hse.gov.uk, gives you access to the latest legislation and you can download a template and create your own H&S policy from the information there.

Having the appropriate insurances in place and setting up a mechanism that keeps you in touch with any legal changes will give you peace of mind and allow you to focus on developing your business.

Risk Assessment

In order to comply with Health & Safety legislation, a business should undertake a risk assessment. This is basically a list of written answers to the question, 'What could go wrong?' It will prepare you for any pitfalls your business is likely to encounter.

General information about the legalities of running a business, including those specific to your industry sector, can be obtained from Business Information Factsheets (BIFs) and Business Opportunity Profiles (BOPs). They are specialist factsheets which are taken from a central database and often your bank or Enterprise Agency will offer them to you. They act as useful guides to the legal aspects of your specific start-up and recommend professional and trade associations which are relevant to your industry. By joining one of these you will be kept up-to-date with legal changes and their insurances are both appropriate and competitively priced.

Business Contracts

Take specialist advice before signing any contracts or legal agreements that you do not fully understand. Contracts are often detailed, complex documents with hidden liabilities which as a layman you might not notice. Leases for rented premises are an example of this.

Leasing premises

Areas to check include:

Length of term - the length of the lease in years and months that you are committed to under the agreement.

If your business does not take off as expected, you may end up paying rent for premises that you no longer use. Similarly, if you are successful but have only signed up for a short lease on a property, you will have to re-negotiate the terms with the landlord early on.

Remember that there are many business premises around to rent and negotiate a flexible deal with a responsible landlord. Discuss what would be best for your business; maybe the incorporation of an early break clause *and* the provision of an extension period could be agreed if the terms are mutually acceptable. Choose a landlord who is sympathetic towards start-ups. As with all contracts, you should aim for a win/win situation where both parties feel happy with what is drawn up.

Responsibility for repairs and insurances

You need to be absolutely clear from the outset which party is responsible for matters such as buildings and contents insurance, repairs and maintenance, and the service charges relating to the premises. Then there is the matter of public liability. Who is liable under the insurance cover if someone has an accident on your leased premises?

Payments in addition to rent, including VAT, service charges, business rates

With rented premises, there are often service charges to pay. These tend to occur when the landlord covers the cost of the building's insurance and the general upkeep and maintenance of the premises. Check that the landlord has given you the full annual rental charge, including service charges, and find out if VAT is payable in addition. Also determine who is responsible for paying the council tax and the utility bills.

If you are unclear about any of the above and the landlord is unwilling to discuss the lease with you, see a solicitor before signing. As with all legal matters, prevention is better than cure.

Terms & Conditions of Business Agreements

Whilst contracts do not always have to be in writing, it is in the interest of any business to have their terms and conditions set out in writing and signed by both parties before any work is undertaken. Disputes arise however fair you are. Without evidence of the terms and conditions you agreed with the other party, they will be time-consuming and expensive to settle. You can research those of a business similar to yours and easily document something along the same lines, before you begin to trade.

Examples of contract situations include:

Buying & Selling Goods & Services

Clear terms and conditions should be attached to any sale of goods or services – even if they are stated under a blanket cover for the whole of your business rather than for individual items.

In the simplest instance, you should declare your returns policy; then there are the complaints procedures, holding of deposits, length of time before payment etc., all of which should be covered in a customer service statement.

Potential customers want to be clear about what buying products and services from you entails; these are your terms and conditions, and in the event of a dispute, such formalities are invaluable.

Hiring and buying equipment on credit

As with leases for business premises, contracts for the hire and credit purchase of items of equipment have obligations that both parties must agree to.

Equipment such fork lift trucks, vans or vehicles – whatever is necessary for your business - will often be bought on credit at start-up. You must be aware of the terms and conditions of any finance agreements. As well as the monthly repayment, finance agreements can contain administration charges, early repayment penalties, and final 'balloon' payments that are often masked in the detail. Early repayment penalties occur if you return the equipment or attempt to cease the agreement before the end of its term. Balloon payments arise at the end of certain contracts when you keep the equipment after the lease period has expired.

It should be clear in the contract which party has ownership of, and responsibility for, the equipment at any stage. Once again, reading the small print is time consuming, but failure to do so might result in high and unexpected costs along the line. Take the time to check the detail.

General automatic implied laws such as the Sale of Goods Act

The government seeks to protect customers from rogue traders and unfair practices. Each town council has an officer in charge of trading standards – visit www.gov.uk/find-local-trading-standards-office for more information.

Your responsibility is to ensure your business is compliant with the regulations. The bottom line is that anything you sell must be of merchantable quality. If a customer finds that any product they purchased from you is faulty or not fit for purpose, they must have access to some form of exchange or refund. Information on product liability can be found on the government website: www.gov.uk/guidance/product-liability-and-safety-law

Franchise and licensing agreements

Companies such as McDonalds, Kwik- Fit, Spar and Subway, all offer their expertise by selling their business models of operation to similar outlets through franchise agreements.

A franchise agreement is made between the franchisor (say McDonalds) and the franchisee (you) and sets out the terms & conditions of working together. The agreement normally entitles you to use the franchisor's business model for advertising, to buy from their suppliers, and to access their administration systems. This is offered in return for an arranged fee and/or a regular payment.

Franchises give you access to proven expertise and are often attractive to start-ups, but there is always an ongoing cost and terms and conditions to adhere to. It is well worth taking specialist advice before embarking on a franchise agreement. You are committing yourself to monthly/annual repayments and often long-term agreements.

Intellectual Property Rights (IPR), copyright, trademarks, design rights, patents, confidentiality agreements

These are complex and confusing areas. The UK Government provides information and guidance, see www.gov.uk/government/organisations/intellectual-property-office

ACID (Anti Copying in Design - www.acid.uk.com) is a trade association that offers advice and guidance on copyright and what to do if your rights appear to be infringed.

In reality, patents and copyright can only go so far in preventing your product or service from being copied. They work, but you have to take legal action against anyone infringing your rights. In practice, protecting copyright can become a never-ending circle of costly lawsuits. Nonetheless, it will work for you as a short-term deterrent.

Innovation and new product development is exciting for everyone, including the government. Leading edge products and technology often result in high profits for the business and high revenues for HMRC from the subsequent taxation.

Entrepreneurs obviously want to protect their

innovations and they look to patents and copyright to do this for them. There are specialist advisers out there to help if you have an innovative product or service – and considerable tax breaks are available for research and development projects. If your product or service is perceived by them as such, they will be glad to offer you professional advice.

Innovators are always (rightly) concerned about others copying their work and, whilst taking precautions through patents, copyright etc. is valuable, sometimes you have to allow market forces to prevail.

In the early days, when your offering is unique and you can charge a high price for it, you will make high profits. If it is later copied by a competitor, entering the market and selling at a lower price, it is inevitable that you will lose some sales - but by then you should have an established and loyal customer base and the ability to use your marketing know-how to fight back.

Business Names

When choosing a name for your business, the legal precedent you should be aware of relates to 'passing off'.

Passing off protects the goodwill of a business from misrepresentation. It prevents a start-up from using the name and imagery of an existing business in a manner that is designed to take away trade from them. For example, if you set up a food outlet that looks like a McDonald's or KFC restaurant, even if you do not use the exact name, the franchisor will sue to stop you trading. As you read earlier, a franchisee has to pay fees to use established branding and business models. It is against the law to operate as one of their chains without entering into a legal agreement with them.

The passing off rule means that you must check any proposed business name, logo and imagery, *before* starting-up. Google it and then look on the Companies House website to check that you will not be legally challenged later by an existing business. A business bank manager will not allow you to open an account in a name that already exists for this reason.

The law works both ways. Once you have your business name, other businesses will not be able to use it. If anyone tries to, as with copyright and patents, it is up to you to stop them – by taking legal action.

Sole traders can use a business name. You do not have to be a limited company to have one, but the passing-off regulations apply to all the legal formats, whichever one you choose.

Employment & Staff Issues

This area has many potential and costly pitfalls. To encourage businesses to take on staff, the government commits significant resources to this area and you can always find help from one of the government's agencies. Recently there have been reductions in National Insurance available to businesses employing people, and free training in Human Resource (HR) Management for growing businesses.

Employing staff is a step-change for a start-up business. The rules and regulations are complex and change regularly – minimum wage, living wage, holiday pay, sickness pay, etc. An employer has to keep on top of all new legislation, although in practice many of them pay for a third party to manage it for them. Government agencies and good accountants offer a great deal of support in this area. They hold seminars on a whole host of topics such as writing job descriptions, interviewing techniques, reference gathering and contracts of employment – everything the owner needs to be aware of.

Online information is also available through the website: www.emplaw.co.uk/ and the Advisory,

Conciliation& Arbitration Service (ACAS) website: www.acas.org.uk/advice

Along with accountants and the government agencies, there are private consultants that offer outsourced HR services. It is worth contacting one of them if you are considering employing staff and are uncertain as to the rules and regulations.

Whilst employing staff is essential in growing a business, in the early stages many start-ups use sub-contract or flexible workers, especially family and friends. This means they avoid the fixed cost of an employee and allows them to wait until the business has reached the point that other people *have* to be brought in before the business can reach its potential.

Secure storage of information and data protection

Holding information carries responsibilities. People's records are confidential and must be treated accordingly. A client database contains personal information which customers give you (they must give you the information willingly - keeping it without their consent contravenes the Data Protection laws) and they expect you to safeguard it. This means you have to have secure storage facilities, both online and offline, when you hold such information.

So..... The legal side of starting and running a business is a potential minefield. The regulations change continually and ignorance is no defence if you break the rules and end up in court. People do manage it successfully – as the next case study shows.

Keeping up-to-date is part of being in business. By signing up to regular newsletters from responsible bodies, or joining a local business network such as the Chamber of Commerce, you will meet other people to share information with and helps you keep abreast of the changes.

Case Study Part 3: Christine Anne Rowlands Beauty & Holistic Therapy

When Christine moved to her own premises she found she had many more legal responsibilities than when she was renting a room.

Leasing business premises

After revising and updating the financial aspects of her business plan, Christine was faced with considering the legal aspects of leasing premises.

The terms of her lease and rental agreement had to be thoroughly reviewed at the outset. This included negotiating on the length of time it covered. Christine had heard of a start-up business in the same locality where the owner arrived for work one morning to find a 'For Sale' notice on the building where his office was. Unbeknown to him, the lease allowed the owner of the building to sell it at any time – something the tenant had not considered when signing up. It made Christine realise that when renting premises, the terms of the lease had to be clearly understood and agreed by both parties in order to avoid any interruption to the business. She studied the lease agreement carefully and only signed it when her landlord agreed to changes she asked for.

Insurances

Christine's lease stated that the landlord was responsible for all of the external aspects of the premises. She would be responsible for the interior and would have to arrange insurance cover for her own property kept on the premises. She considered the terms and conditions of several insurance policies and when she eventually chose a provider, she set about ensuring that she complied with their conditions as she knew that the insurance company would only agree to a claim if she conformed to the standards set out in the policy.

Having the best and most appropriate insurances was essential in Christine's business. She required cover for the following:

Contents insurance

Public Liability insurance - to cover the cost of any claims which might be brought against her for accidents on her premises

Employer Liability insurance - to cover the cost of any legal claims by or against an employee

Motor vehicle insurance - cover for business use, for example, if she was involved in an accident whilst travelling to her suppliers

Christine found the best cover and most competitive price through the trade association she had membership with, the Federation of Holistic Therapists. Federations, professional and trade associations offer their members insurances specifically designed for their industry and as Christine says, benefits such as this are well worth the membership fees.

Planning permission & Local Authority conditions

As Christine's premises had formerly been used for residential purposes, she had to apply to the Local Authority for change of use to business.

This involved several meetings with council officers and the updating of her business plan, for their purposes. Certain conditions were stipulated, including providing disabled access. She also learned that because the area was partly residential, neon signs were prohibited and her opening hours were restricted (trading was not permitted after 8pm each evening or on Sundays). The A-board she used for advertising was not allowed outside the new premises as it was a public footpath, but Christine got round this by positioning it on the grass verge on the opposite side of the path.

Throughout the conversion of the premises she was regularly inspected to ensure that she was complying with the regulations. Although Christine found this demanding and had to make several trips to the Town Hall, she says that the people were extremely helpful towards her.

Licences & other legal obligations

Once the lease was signed and the conversion accepted by the Local Authority, Christine looked at the operation of business in terms of the legal necessities that ensured her insurances were effective. She found she needed several licences, including the following:

A licence to use needles for electrolysis treatments; she had to register with the Environmental Health Department for this. There was an initial cost for the licence and a subsequent annual fee.

A licence to play CD's in the treatment rooms; she needed a music licence to comply with the broadcasting and performing rights regulations and if she used her computer to watch television at any time, she would also need a TV licence. She later found there were certain recordings made by artists who were not members of the Performing Rights Society and that she could play these without a licence.

Portable Appliance (PAT) testing was required for all her electrical appliances at the outset and at three year intervals afterwards.

An accident book had to be maintained in case insurance claims were brought against her.

Any personal data had to be securely saved and stored to ensure client confidentiality.

Employing staff

When Christine revised her business plan she did not intend to employ staff. Now she has two employees.

Both moving to her own premises and employing staff have been serious decisions for Christine. She was always determined to have enough customers before taking any steps to grow her business.

Her first employee was her daughter. Like many family businesses, she brought in someone she trusted and could communicate with easily.

Her second employee was the nail technician who rented a room from her on a self-employed basis.

When her tenant's family commitments changed and she found she was struggling to promote and manage her own business, she decided to look for employed part-time work. She approached Christine first. By this time the clients requiring nail treatments were growing fast and Christine had developed a good working relationship with her. She decided to employ her on a part-time basis, rather than have her leave the business.

With the increased responsibility of employees, Christine approached her accountant. For an additional fee, he added a payroll package to her range of services. Now, if she is unsure of anything, she just picks up the phone and calls him.

Business names

Christine, like many other traders, spent a lot of time considering a name for her business. Each one she liked was already in use, and when a member of her family asked what was wrong with using her own name as it appeared to work for many other successful businesses, she decided to go for it.

Chapter 10: Management Information

When businesses grow, employing staff becomes inevitable. From then onwards the owner has to learn how to delegate, whilst retaining control of the business.

As an owner/manager you survive by knowing what is happening both in your business and in the market. When you employ people and they take on some of your responsibilities, it's easy to lose touch.

Effective delegation involves setting out what you want from your employees and receiving feedback from them as to what is happening in practice. Successful businesses gradually develop systems which include information as to the performance of each key area of the business. The simplest system measures weekly or monthly sales and expenses – customer sales, profitability and cash flow being the driving forces of all businesses.

In time, the need for information grows and more formal systems – known as Management Information Systems (MIS) – have to be introduced. These systems do exactly what the name suggests - they give the owner information on the areas he or she has delegated. This is gathered and recorded and used as the focus for regular team meetings where the current position of the business is discussed and plans to move forward are developed.

Setting up a system

Established businesses have monthly, fortnightly or weekly management meetings. Along with financial information such as the Profit & Loss Account, there should be other measurements of progress reported, for example:

Product/service sales information – broken down into categories which allow the business to find the most and least successful selling lines

Stock and distribution information – on time or late deliveries; stock shortages or excesses; any relevant supplier information such as increased charges or discounts

Marketing information – number of enquiries; conversion of enquiries to sales; returns / complaints by product / service category; number of new customers; number of repeat customers; competitor information; advertising costs........ and any other specific measures of performance.

As your business grows, your MIS will enable you to delegate whilst remaining in control. To begin with, you need to know what sells best and which areas make most profit. One level up and it becomes all about customers – finding new ones and retaining existing ones.

Back-up / storage of information

One of the reasons businesses fail is because they lose their information.

When you start out in business you keep a lot of information in your head and often act on instinct. Then you begin to record transactions because: a) you have to for tax purposes and b) you simply can't remember everything. Backing up your records is a priority - yet many start-ups fail to do so.

Cloud backup provides an automatic means of protecting your computerised data. There are many systems on the market and you should choose the most reliable, even if you have to pay for it. As with insurance, it will be worth it. Through encryption your data will be secured and this means that you will be in compliance with the Data Protection regulations. One of the main ways to lose your clients is to give away their details; make sure that both computerised and documented date is always safely stored.

Unless you are an accountant, it is unlikely that you will be able to set up an all-singing, all-dancing set of management information – and you don't need to. Keep a simple recording system that highlights the key performance areas of your business - your Key Performance Indicators (KPI's). Design a simple layout and update the figures regularly.

There is a well-known saying in business, 'Don't expect what you don't inspect'. Management information systems are essential if you delegate - they keep the business on (your) track.

Chapter 11: And finally……

You should now have enough information to help you decide if you want to test a business idea or step out into self-employment. Even if it is not your first choice, and you would prefer to be employed, you now know the basic financial and legal facts that govern a start-up business – whether it's full-time, part-time or a combination. You know how to set up and where to look for help and advice. It's also important to remember that you will learn as you go along.

A recession or downturn can be the perfect time for starting up in business. People with money to spend are looking for alternatives - products and services that offer great value for money. If you find a gap in the market - where competition is weak - it could be the perfect time for you to make your entrance.

This book is your foundation, but don't stop here. Go to the support agencies and get as much help and advice as you can. Keep up with the legal side by networking. Test the market before you commit your precious resources; this is how you find out how to sell yourself and your products or services.

Keep the magic formula:

'Sales minus Expenses equals Profit or Loss'

at the forefront of your mind - and watch your cash flow continuously.

If starting-up is your dream, good luck with your venture and thank you for reading this book. I hope it has motivated and inspired you to move your business idea forward.

About my books

You will have gathered by now that as a Business Adviser, Trainer & Mentor in Finance & Marketing, I have a passion for start-ups. I've worked with them and growth businesses for over 20 years.

From the workshops I've delivered, I know that the financial and legal issues −particularly raising finance and dealing with the taxman − are what people want to know about initially. Then, once they've got to grips with these, they realise that what they've learned won't actually bring in any customers and they want information about marketing.

If you've found this book useful, maybe you'd like to take a look at my marketing text. It includes case studies of how Christine Anne Rowlands and other successful businesses marketed their enterprises right from the start.

Contact the Author

Reviews are so important to an author and I would greatly appreciate it if you could take the time to post a review on Amazon.

Join me on Facebook;
www.facebook.com/eileenhirst - author/

Or on Twitter;
www.twitter.com/eileenhirst/

I hope you have found the information useful and helpful and I wish you every success in your business venture.

Eileen Hirst

Printed in Great Britain
by Amazon